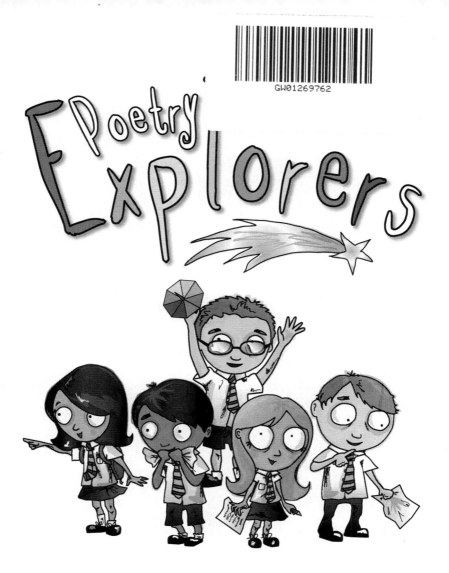

Poetry Explorers

South & West London
Edited by Donna Samworth

First published in Great Britain in 2009 by

Remus House
Coltsfoot Drive
Peterborough
PE2 9JX
Telephone: 01733 890066
Website: www.youngwriters.co.uk

All Rights Reserved
Book Design by Spencer Hart
Illustrations by Ali Smith
© Copyright Contributors 2009
SB ISBN 978-1-84924-306-3

Foreword

At Young Writers our defining aim is to promote an enjoyment of reading and writing amongst children and young adults. By giving aspiring poets the opportunity to see their work in print, their love of the written word as well as confidence in their own abilities has the chance to blossom.

Our latest competition, Poetry Explorers, was designed to introduce primary school children to the wonders of creative expression. They were given free reign to write on any theme and in any style, thus encouraging them to use and explore a variety of different poetic forms.

We are proud to present the resulting collection of regional anthologies which are an excellent showcase of young writing talent. With such a diverse range of entries received, the selection process was difficult yet very rewarding. From comical rhymes to poignant verses, there is plenty to entertain and inspire within these pages. We hope you agree that this collection bursting with imagination is one to treasure.

Contents

Castlecombe Primary School, Mottingham

- Olivia Smithson (8) 1
- Alfie Read-Fulcher (7) 1
- Zak Jones (9) 2
- Elisha Kudaisi (10) 2
- Jamie Wilson (10) 3
- Chloe Quayle (10) 3
- Danny Jeacock (7) 4
- Billy Burns (8) 4
- Katarna Roper (8) 5
- Jack Ellis (8) 5
- Alfie Tilley (8) 6
- Rachel Nash (8) 6
- Luke Harvie (7) 7
- Davisha Gopee Singh (8) 7
- James Penfold (8) 8
- Emily Cox (9) 8
- Alfie Whiting (9) 9
- Femi Oni-Orisan (10) 9
- Ellie Tripp (8) 10
- Amy-May Derrick (7) 10
- Orhan Turkoglu (10) 11
- Harry Bolt (8) 11
- Dylan Bouskill (8) 11
- Katie Clint (8) 12
- Morgan Brown (10) 12
- Tarik Bucknall (9) 12

Henry Cavendish Primary School, Balham

- Nur Khan (8) 13
- Rita Mably (8) 14
- Lauren Peaty-Da'Silva (8) 14
- Ellie Amy Griffiths (9) 15
- Holly Platt (9) 15
- Zaynah Charles (10) 16

- Charlie Sayers (9) & Rosie Hooper (10) 16
- Charles David Lawrence (9) 17
- Amber Sheehan & Theá Blais (9) 17
- Dominic Manto (10) 18
- Alisha (7) 18
- Rosanna Lainé Webster (9) 19
- Victoria Byiers-Oldfield (9) 19
- Karis Knight 20
- Hannah Rosa Everitt (8) 20
- Isabella Massey (9) 21
- Carla Rose Cole (9) 21
- Charis Gates & Elaine Traykov (9) 22
- Lola Snow (8) 22

Ivydale Primary School, Nunhead

- Tyler Guthrie (11) 23
- Mohima Ahmed (8) 23
- Edward Obelley (11) 24
- Daniel Thompson-Wallace (11) 24
- Layla Issaka (10) 25
- Wilf Hutchings (10) 25
- Lauren Thurston (10) 26
- Emelia Findlay (9) 26
- Sarah Benneworth (11) 27
- Tia Hassan (9) 27
- Molly Joan Turrell (10) 28
- Tyra Lafayette 28
- Darelle Hernandez (10) 29
- Tia Briscoe-Alexander (9) 29
- Nell Amos (8) 30
- Willard Richards-Gray (8) 30
- Sade Rasheda Mavoka (10) 31
- Joe Ward (10) 31
- Harriet Arinze (11) 32
- N'Tanya Clark (10) 32
- Karen Annang (11) 33

Nina Solomon (10) 33
Max Rampton (9) 34
Chloe Sweet (10) 34
Layla Chaudhury-Laird (8) 35
Marie-Louise Beatrice Jugant (9) 35
Harry Surey (10) 36
Theodore Jugant (8) 36

Kingswood Primary School, Lambeth

Ella Tshibambi-Niles (10) 37
Zara Wilson (8) 38
Rasses-Senami Attolou (10) 39
Reann Harrison (11) 39

Linton Mead Primary School, Thamesmead

Tiffany Ndukwe (11) 40
Nadia Szoma (9) 40
Vlad Miclaus (9) 41
Nicholas Eker-Moura (8) 41
Fatimah Mohd-Fauzi (8) 42
Nathaniel Olalekan (9) 42
Ore Akin-Odidi (10) 43
Abayomi Olawale Lawal (9) 43
Habeeb Periklis Lawal (9) 44
Oreoluwa Ola Kareem (10) 44
Siti Nur Syakirah Mohd-Fauzi (10) 45
Aliyah Miah (7) 45
Chloe Kiernan (9) 46
Folarin Aina (9) 46
Amy Elizabeth Honour & Deborah Afolabi (9) 47
Hannah Jones (8) 47
Kelvin Ihama (8) 48
Oyindamola Adelaiye (8) 48
Sacha Waite (8) 49
Lois Ann Moore (8) 49
Oyindamola Onasanya (8) 50
Poppy Howes (8) 50
Sasha Roots (8) 50
Michelle Ndukwe (9) 51
Laura Umoh (7) 51

Jason Poon (9) 51
Liam Dand (8) 52

Little Ealing Primary School, Ealing

Jennie Connelly (9) 53
Jennie Connelly & Carys Hindry (9) 54
Maiya Harrison-Genis (8) 55

North Ealing Primary School, Ealing

Ravi Dhillon (9) 56
Anishaa Pattani (8) 57
Deena Ahmed (9) 58
Jago Di Piro (9) 58
Chloe Kenway (8) 59
Showgo Kimuna (9) 59
Kai Wing 60
Freya Gann (8) 60
Abigail Bean (8) 61
James Bartle (9) 61
Matthew Hughes (9) 62
Lucy Henfield (9) 62
Maisie Backshall (8) 63
Zak Lyons (9) 63
Ranil West 64
James Cogan-Tucker (8) 64
Kiara Lorenzo (8) 65
Parsa Sarkis (9) 65
Lucy Bagot (10) 66
Romain Potier (9) 66
Finn Byrne (8) 67

Peter Hills School, Rotherhithe

Thomas Long (10) 67
Sam Brooks-Martin (10) 68
Khamille Gordon (9) 69
Rebecca Evans 69
Brooke Morgan (9) 70
Remy Soares (9) 70
Bobbi Tassell (10) 71
Carlotta Falsetti-Flatt (8) 71
Maddison Clancy (8) 72

Ayomide Dina (9)	72
Jamie Smith (9)	73
Ajay Fadeyi (10)	73
Monique Brodie-Mends (10)	74
Ellie Segar (9)	74

Robin Hood Primary School, Kingston Vale

Edward Paterson (8)	75
Lauren Sheree Edwards (8)	76
Tharushi S Bhagya Denipitiya (8)	76
Emma Hall (8)	77

St Anne's RC Primary School, Vauxhall

Renée Osaze Eguavoen (9)	78

St Benedict's Junior School, Ealing

Milo Rose (10)	78
Bethany Porter (9)	79
Alvin Lee (10)	80
Philip Byrnes (7)	80
Shane Duffy (8)	81
Edward Sullivan (9)	81
Casimir Bowyer (11)	82
Thomas Zussman (8)	82
Finn Hobson (10)	83
Cristina Moran (9)	83
Hector Hardman (10)	84
Gabriel Kerr (8)	84
Dominic King (11)	85
Stefan Serkilar (8)	85
Tobias Campbell (9)	86
Luke Cassidy (9)	86
Katherine Reid (10)	87
Alexander Hughes (9)	87
Edward Hansell (8)	88
Patrick Edis (9)	88
Joss Bell (9)	89
Madeleine Harris (8)	89
Eddie Szlachetko (8)	90
Lorcan O'Brien (9)	90

Robert Drepaul (8)	91
Isabella Wingrave (9)	91
Jordan Bedeau (10)	92
George Charlesworth (8)	92
Rachel de Cintra (9)	93
Thomas Goode (8)	93
Sam Loveless (11)	94
Christopher Pullen (10)	94
Liam Carty-Howe (9)	95
Tristan Jenkin-Gomez (9)	95
Lewis Cox (9)	96
Ellie Scott (10)	96
Sam Lubkowski (10)	97
James Worrall (8)	97
Charles Ayson Parrish (9)	98
Luke Rutherford (8)	98
Freddie Greenwood (9)	99
Theodore Hyams (8)	99
Billy Oubridge (9)	100
James Ball (7)	100
Binath Philomin (8)	101
Camena Foote (9)	101
Henry Weathersbee (9)	101

St John's CE Primary School, Penge

Krista Yaxley (9)	102
India Barrett (7)	102
Chloe Cornish (10)	103
Darius Xavier (7)	103
Rachel Langford Honeysett (9)	104
Alana Hewitt (10)	104
Joseph Adusei	105
Clare Symons (11)	105
Ella Robertson	106
Olivia Tizie (9)	106

St John's CE Primary School, Walworth

Alicia Treleven (11)	106
Ben Fox (11)	107
Gift Okonkwo (11)	108
Tamara Ajudua (11)	109
Tyanna McLean (11)	110

Tosin Sokoya (10) 111
Paris McLean (10) 111
Brian Asiedu-Obiri (11) 112

Sheen Mount School, Sheen

Millie Price (8) 112
Georgina Russell (8) 113
Harriet Groves (8) 113

Stockwell Primary School, Lambeth

Vincent Wong 114
Osman Sihaam 114
Rasidatu Bisuga (6) 115
Aaron Ormsby 115
Mateusz Matczak (9) 116
Fahima Khatun 116
Jamith Horna 117
Rachel Wong (9) 117
Aaliya Mohamed 118
Diogo 118
Nadiyah Hazari 119

Sulivan Primary School, Fulham

Ahlam Nur (9) 119
Hoda Tarmach (8) 120
Samuel James Constanti (9) 121
Amal Jama (8) 122
Jonathan Kyle (7) 122
Angel Lawal (7) 123
James Gent (10) 123
Brooke Blagrove (9) 124

The Priory CE Primary School, Wimbledon

Indiana Fofie-Collins (8) 124
Joe Sansom (9) 125
Devendra Bathia (9) 126
Kyle Sterling (8) 126
Gabriel Tweedale (9) 127
Joseph Digger (8) 127

Kayleigh Spencer Smyth (8) 128

The Poems

Poetry Explorers – South & West London

A Mermaid's Paradise

Deep down in the blue sapphire sea
the mermaids play happy and free,
they dance and sing until they can do no more.

On the jewel-encrusted ocean floor
the jellyfish and lobsters play hide-and-seek
while the big fish swim by with their big white teeth.

Up to the surface the mermaids swim
laughing and twirling towards the sun.
As they bask upon the ragged rocks
they comb their long, flowing, golden locks.

Over the horizon the fishing boats come
to spoil the mermaids' fun in the sun.
'Come on girls, it's time to go.'
But they will be back tomorrow, you know.

Olivia Smithson (8)
Castlecombe Primary School, Mottingham

Animals

A t the farm I met a goat
N aughty goat, he ate my coat
I n the field I saw a cow
M aking funny noises, *wow!*
A t the zoo I saw a lion
L uckily he didn't eat Brian
S sh! What's that? I think it's a snake,
                        run for it!

Alfie Read-Fulcher (7)
Castlecombe Primary School, Mottingham

Sounds

Car engines revving
Water dripping
Lions roaring
Babies crying
Dogs barking
People screaming
Elephants stomping
Music playing
People clapping
Rivers splashing
Builders working
These are some sounds we can hear.

Zak Jones (9)
Castlecombe Primary School, Mottingham

Space

Space is a beautiful place,
It is very dark.
When you look at all the stars,
They put a smile on your face.
If you look at all the stars,
They seem very small,
But really they are very big,
But not as big as Mars.
Big, small, bumpy, rough.
The planets are all different,
But all beautiful in their way.
None full of fluff!

Elisha Kudaisi (10)
Castlecombe Primary School, Mottingham

Time Travel

T ime
I n space
M ega-big vortex
E ach mysterious

T ime machine
R un by plutonium
A nd
V ortex
E xtremely dangerous
L ike a black hole.

Jamie Wilson (10)
Castlecombe Primary School, Mottingham

The Jungle

T igers roar roaming through the jungle.
H owler monkeys howling loud
E lephant with its great big tusks.

J umping from tree to tree, yeah, they're monkeys.
U nmissable lion, king of the jungle.
N on-stoppable cheetah.
G orilla going crazy.
L eaves falling from trees
E verybody loves animals.

Chloe Quayle (10)
Castlecombe Primary School, Mottingham

Football

F un and fast
O n the grass
O ut to win
T he other team
B all you need
A ll the time
L ots of fun
L iverpool is the best.

Danny Jeacock (7)
Castlecombe Primary School, Mottingham

Football

F ootball is my favourite game.
O ver the goal goes the ball.
O ur team is called Leeford.
T ackling is sometimes rough.
B all control is important.
A ll the parents cheer us on.
L ee Ford is the best.
L ee is my brother's coach.

Billy Burns (8)
Castlecombe Primary School, Mottingham

Katarna

K atarna is a banana
A fantastic girl
T he girl who likes fashion
A girl who likes animals
R ed is her favourite colour
N obody's like her
A talented girl who loves to twirl.

Katarna Roper (8)
Castlecombe Primary School, Mottingham

Octopus

O ctopus has eight legs
C an swim in the sea
T hey are like squids
O n the bottom of the sea
P eople like them
U nder the sea
S wimming happily.

Jack Ellis (8)
Castlecombe Primary School, Mottingham

The Sea

T he waves crash and smash
H ere live lots of creatures
E ach one swimming as fast as they can

S harks, octopuses and starfish
E very one of them loves the waves
A nd splashing around in the sea.

Alfie Tilley (8)
Castlecombe Primary School, Mottingham

The Sparkling Sea

T he wonderful sea is splashing for me.
H ear the waves go *whoosh, whoosh.*
E ach grain of sand sparkles like diamonds.

S mell the salty air in the breeze.
E very seagull sings a song.
A n amazing beach is great for me.

Rachel Nash (8)
Castlecombe Primary School, Mottingham

Sharks

S harks are my favourite fish
H iding in the sea
A nd they eat fish too
R arely seen in England
K illing fish is their favourite hobby
S o that's why I like sharks.

Luke Harvie (7)
Castlecombe Primary School, Mottingham

Monkeys

M onkeys eat yummy bananas.
O n the trees they swing.
N ear the jungle they live,
K eeping their baby monkeys safe.
E ating when they're hungry.
Y elling when other animals run after them.

Davisha Gopee Singh (8)
Castlecombe Primary School, Mottingham

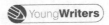

Monkeys

M y favourite is a chimpanzee.
O rang-utans are hairy.
N aughty monkeys show their bottoms.
K ieron thinks they're scary.
E very zoo has a monkey.
Y ou can see them if you pay with money.

James Penfold (8)
Castlecombe Primary School, Mottingham

Karate

K icks, punches and blocks.
A good Karta gets me graded.
R ed belt nearly.
A ll about self-defence.
T eaches discipline.
E verybody's having fun.

Emily Cox (9)
Castlecombe Primary School, Mottingham

Acrostic Hobbies

B oxing is a great sport, no doubt.
O pponents you have to beat.
X -rays are for bad conditions
I f you get hurt.
N eeds training.
G oing home now because we're finished.

Alfie Whiting (9)
Castlecombe Primary School, Mottingham

The Jungle

J aguars searching for their prey.
U nder the mud lie sliding snakes.
N octurnal creatures sleeping in the day.
G ullible baboons in the sun.
L ovely koala bears eating eucalyptus leaves.
E lephants stomping out of control.

Femi Oni-Orisan (10)
Castlecombe Primary School, Mottingham

Horses

H uggable and cuddly.
O utstandingly gentle.
R unning and galloping around.
S unning themselves in the field.
E ating hay in their stables.
S leeping in a soft, deep bed.

Ellie Tripp (8)
Castlecombe Primary School, Mottingham

Lions

L ions are great.
I love lions.
O n rocks lions sleep.
N oisy lions
S houting to their cubs.

Amy-May Derrick (7)
Castlecombe Primary School, Mottingham

Space

S tars twinkling in the skylight.
P lanets that rockets zoom past.
A stronauts flying past, all around up in space.
C omets flying all around space.
E very planet that you've ever seen.

Orhan Turkoglu (10)
Castlecombe Primary School, Mottingham

Beach

B eing on the beach is fun.
E ating ice creams with a Flake.
A lways making sandcastles.
C ollecting empty shells.
H igh waves with surfers on.

Harry Bolt (8)
Castlecombe Primary School, Mottingham

Lion

Lion, king of the jungle.
Monkeys running by.
Clouds in the sky.
I am scared.
Lion roaring.

Dylan Bouskill (8)
Castlecombe Primary School, Mottingham

Elephants

Elephants are big and strong
With big ears and a long nose
They eat a lot
They play in water
To cool down.

Katie Clint (8)
Castlecombe Primary School, Mottingham

Space

S tars
P lanets whizzing all around
A stronauts in their spaceships
C omets
E very planet you've ever seen.

Morgan Brown (10)
Castlecombe Primary School, Mottingham

The Earth

S tars shining in the sky
P lanets are everywhere
A stronaut
C entre of the Earth
E arth is where we live.

Tarik Bucknall (9)
Castlecombe Primary School, Mottingham

I Am Who I Am

I am who I am, because of my loving educational caring, handsome dad.
I am who I am because of the amazing job my dad has.
I am who I am because of my loving, caring, pretty, beautiful, yummy, food-making, wonderful mum.
I am who I am because of my clever dad who teaches me my times tables.
I am who I am because of my biggest sister who teaches me how to stand up for myself.
I am who I am because of my second biggest sister who teaches me how to read and write stories with lots of describing words.
I am who I am because of my cute, smiley, giggly little sister.
I am who I am because of my pretty, beautiful, kind teacher, Miss Walker.
I am who I am because of my pretty, kind, nice and caring teacher, Miss Moore, who made history my second-best subject, last year.
I am who I am because of my teacher, Miss Ekins who taught me in reception; she encouraged me to go on a school trip to the zoo.
I am who I am because of my teacher, Miss Harper, who taught me in Year 1, she improved my handwriting.
I am who I am because of the support my family gives me.
I am who I am because of the support my class gives me.
I am who I am because of my friends who play with me when I am lonely.
I am who I am because of my religion.
I am who I am because of what I want to be, a gymnast and a doctor.
I am who I am because of my talent.
I am who I am because of my memory of my old house.
I am who I am because of everyone.

Nur Khan (8)
Henry Cavendish Primary School, Balham

New Moon

When the new moon shines down,
the light beams in my eyes,
like a tiger hunting for his prey.

When the new moon shines down,
I see nothing but sparks of light,
flashing wildly in the dark midnight sky.

When the new moon shines down,
the ground looks like a sea of sparkles,
gleaming and twinkling, looking right at me.

When the new moon shines down,
I hear no noise just the whistling of the wind
and the lapping of the waves.

When the new moon shines down . . .
When the new moon shines down . . .

Rita Mably (8)
Henry Cavendish Primary School, Balham

Tiger

I am fire
Orange and black
Like the blackout sky
So dark you can't see a thing.
My tail swings
Through the green bright grass,
Tickling occasionally.
My paws bound through the jungle.

Lauren Peaty-Da'Silva (8)
Henry Cavendish Primary School, Balham

The Wild Swan

His feathers are as white as snow
His face is as black as soot
Every day his elegance grows
He has a webbed foot.

He flies across the water like a boat
His beak is as orange as a fish
He has a beautiful white coat
He has a meal but no dish.

He leads the elegant row at the top
He has a wonderful crown
His magic never stops
The other animals bow down.

He is the swan as beautiful as can be
He is as free as you and me.

Ellie Amy Griffiths (9)
Henry Cavendish Primary School, Balham

Tiger

Something flickers in the night,
Vicious and valiant, it prowls through the bushes.
Fur like fire and coal, it shocks you with its growling.
A serious animal on the hunt.
Travelling around at its own pace,
Eyes dark brown, bold and blazing.
Its teeth as sharp as arrowheads and shining white.
The strong body swerves from side to side as it goes on its hunt.

Holly Platt (9)
Henry Cavendish Primary School, Balham

Song

This, that, I give and take,
This, that, I keep and break,
Is and is, not my own
But lives in itself, alone,
Yet, is between us two,
Mine only in the breaking,
It's all in the remaking,
Doing what I undo.

With it all must be well
They were the invisible
So be it between us two
A giving be our taking
A making our unmaking
A doing what we undo.

Zaynah Charles (10)
Henry Cavendish Primary School, Balham

A Poem About Me

Everybody likes me - I guess I'm just likeable
Except my big sister who thinks that I'm horrible
I'm perfect in every way but sadly I'm not loveable
My teacher always tells me that I must learn my twelve times table
I never knew that soap was inedible
Until I ate it
And got bubbles in my mouth which made me very bounceable
My favourite board game has to be Scrabble
And I also think that maths is really terrible.

Charlie Sayers (9) & Rosie Hooper (10)
Henry Cavendish Primary School, Balham

Poetry Explorers – South & West London

Fire

As
it looks
at the dark
with a devilish
smile, as it spreads
light across the world,
as it licks at the water
screaming for help, as
if it were a child playing by
the sandy shore. As it stomps
over forests and trees penetrating
whatever it spots in its gaze.
Fire!

Charles David Lawrence (9)
Henry Cavendish Primary School, Balham

The Shimmering Snowflakes – Haikus

The snow is falling
Whizzing, whirling, floating down
The winter is here.

Snowballs are flying
They smash hard against the ground
They break into bits.

The school is now closed
Because of the falling snow
We all say, 'Wahoo!'

Amber Sheehan & Theá Blais (9)
Henry Cavendish Primary School, Balham

The World (Earth)

As I look high in the sky,
When shooting stars zoom by
I ask myself, 'Why is there crime and violence, why?'

People should be kind, filled with love,
And be harmless, innocent, just like a dove,
We should live in a clean, smiling world,
Where no one is criticising another in any place.

Can Earth change?
Can Earth be a good planet to live on?
Can I say that Earth is a sweet, loving place
Where everyone is happy?

Earth! Earth! Earth!

Dominic Manto (10)
Henry Cavendish Primary School, Balham

Hot Potato!

P otatoes big, potatoes small, we love them all
O is the shape of a potato
T o America and back
A tasty spud for dinner
T o the finish line, yeah, it's the winner
O h no, the blight has come
E veryone's potato is black and dead
S leep, oh great potatoes, sleep.

Alisha (7)
Henry Cavendish Primary School, Balham

Romance Poem

You are mine
Till we're dead
Day in, day out
We are still wed.

We are together
We're like doves
For when we're together
We're in love!

When you say a joke
You make me cry
For when you kiss me,
I float up to the sky!

Rosanna Lainé Webster (9)
Henry Cavendish Primary School, Balham

The Tiger

As its eyes twinkle in the dark, dark night,
Thump, thump go its paws when it slaps them down
On the wet, greasy grass.
It gives the animals a big, big fright,
It is so totally first class.
The black on it really stands out,
When animals see it, they don't hang about!

Victoria Byiers—Oldfield (9)
Henry Cavendish Primary School, Balham

Railway Dog

I sit or lie right next to the railway
Watching the trains go puffing by
But all I can ever do is sigh

People stare at me as they zoom past
But I never get a look in because it is so fast

For a drink I wish
But in a family I miss

I sit by the railway
Because I'm a railway dog

I never get bored though
My head never to be low.

Karis Knight
Henry Cavendish Primary School, Balham

The Sea

The wonderful, wavy sea, crashing and smashing against the rocks,
Glittering and twinkling on a starry, dark, black night.
Every day you see the sea come scuttling into the shore,
Carrying people from continent to continent.
Boats getting smaller and smaller as they cross the horizon,
Bringing happiness to people who love swimming and splashing
                              in the turquoise water.
Washing stones and pretty shells ready to decorate the sand,
And giving safety and care to lots of strange sea creatures.

Wavy, glittering, crashing, smashing, twinkling . . .
It's the sea!

Hannah Rosa Everitt (8)
Henry Cavendish Primary School, Balham

My Vain Tail!

I'm as black as coal and as orange as marmalade,
I swish my vain tail,
My ear-blowing roar travels for miles,
I hunt for my prey every day,
As I flicker my fur, my eyes go a dark brown,
My long, slippery tongue curls up.

I'm bold and serious as an angry head teacher,
My eyesight is an excellent thing,
Shock,
I eat like a hungry lion,
Growling like mad,
My paws stamp away.

Isabella Massey (9)
Henry Cavendish Primary School, Balham

Happiness

Happiness is having friends that smile at you every day.
Happiness is sending back a friendly smile.
Happiness is picking up a fallen friend.
Happiness is reaching out to a friendly and lonely soul.
Happiness, happiness is what you make it.
Happiness is for each and every one.

Carla Rose Cole (9)
Henry Cavendish Primary School, Balham

Celebrations

Bang, sizzle, pop, fireworks exploding, flashing,
me standing looking at all the bright colours.

All the amazing coloured costumes of birds, animals,
dragons, heroes, everything you know.

Magic worlds all around me like a single wind in a huge storm.
While the music plays, I sway gently to the great sound
of the loud cheer of people.

Silence stops everybody, the grand finale;
a multicoloured blur of fireworks explode in the sky
in the shape of the English flag
and a roar of cheers spread through the crowd.

Charis Gates & Elaine Traykov (9)
Henry Cavendish Primary School, Balham

Lola

L avender is pale mauve.
O range blossom is orange.
L ilies mostly come in white,
A nd put them together, they are rainbow bright!

Lola Snow (8)
Henry Cavendish Primary School, Balham

I Will Never Forget You

Remember me when I am gone away
Silent thoughts lie in your brain
Thinking of me brings you pain
May we meet anew on a summer's day

Sleep sweetly my first ever love
Dream deeply of when we first did meet
I opened my arms to take my heart seat
I reminisce of you when I see a dove

Remember me when I leave this town
Take this basket to represent my feelings
I hope when I come back, your heart will be healing
You have invested our love, it's true
When I come back you can choose a smile or a frown
And this is why I will never forget you.

Tyler Guthrie (11)
Ivydale Primary School, Nunhead

Sadness Is . . .

The colour black and grey.
Tastes of salt.
Is the sound of people crying.
Is not nice.
Is the symbol of crying.
Feels like a lonely place.
Is like an empty playground.
Is a lonely feeling.
Sadness is a terrible thing.

Mohima Ahmed (8)
Ivydale Primary School, Nunhead

My Past

Remember me when I am gone away
Gone far away, away from you
Where our soft, pure love will never be true
Never turning back, for my mistake must pay
Remember me on that bright sunny day
Where as we leave our past in fog and mist
Nevertheless I remember the day we first kissed
You will always be in my head as I lie
Yet if a tear should roll down your cheek
Do not feel sorrow as I will always be single
You will always make my heart tingle
If, for once, you forget me
My will, will grow weak
And I will surely die, you'll see!

Edward Obelley (11)
Ivydale Primary School, Nunhead

Umbrellas

Underneath, keeping dry.
Me, my mates and I.
Black clouds block out the sky.
Rain pours down on passers-by.
Eyes on feet, puddles missed.
Lightning strikes the soggy ground.
Ladies' legs covered in drizzle.
Angry ants floating by.
Sky clears, we all heave a sigh.

Daniel Thompson-Wallace (11)
Ivydale Primary School, Nunhead

Love Forgotten

Remember me when I am gone away
Gone into a land lovely and bright
So I may find a wife, I really might
And in a lovely house, I will always stay
Maybe, like children, we were bonny and gay
Don't grieve for me, you must understand
That you may never take me by the hand
Or keep me company on a cold winter's day
Our days together were so nice
But for the two of us, it's just not right
For we may even argue, or worse, fight
I'd be filled with guilt if you were sad
My heart is not as hard as ice
I will weep heartbreakingly for what we once had.

Layla Issaka (10)
Ivydale Primary School, Nunhead

Umbrella

When the rain trickles and water falls
You can only rely on an umbrella
An umbrella's like a magnificent shield
Given by factories
That stops the rain from falling on you
Waterproof clothes, no need for that
You can always rely on an umbrella
My umbrella is orange and black
It's got soaking wet so I have put it on a rack.

Wilf Hutchings (10)
Ivydale Primary School, Nunhead

Remember Me Forever

Remember me when I am gone away
Gone far away to be a Christian wife
It is my only wish in life
Yet I dearly wish to stay
You shall never be my honey
I will never forget you
You love me, I know you do
But my father knows you lack the money
You are my true love to say the least
I have learned to treasure what I have
And I would hate to see you sad
So shall I come back? No, never!
Please do not give me grief
Despite what's happened, I will love you forever.

Lauren Thurston (10)
Ivydale Primary School, Nunhead

The Rain Poem

I like rain,
Because I am insane,
It doesn't usually come to Spain.
The birds in the sky,
Can no longer fly,
One even gets some rain in its eye.
Rain is fun,
Not as much as the sun,
It isn't very nice at all, hon!

Emelia Findlay (9)
Ivydale Primary School, Nunhead

True Love

Remember me when I am gone away
When my life has gone to a loving land
Now, me and you cannot touch hands
I will now stay on this summer's day
Me and you were like two turtle doves
Now me and you are through
Yet I dearly love you
You really were my first ever love
I will never forget you
All these loving tears
Are coming from so many lovely years
You make me cry with your smile
I really do love you
But just leave me alone for a while.

Sarah Benneworth (11)
Ivydale Primary School, Nunhead

Snowy Days

Snow is falling in the air
Snow is falling everywhere
Snow is melting on the ground
Snow goes back around
Snow is cold and it's white
Snow is crispy and it's bright
Snow is slippery when it's ice
Snow is very nice.

Tia Hassan (9)
Ivydale Primary School, Nunhead

Umbrellas

Spotty and dotty,
Splashes and slashes,
Square or round,
Ten or one pound,
Drip,
Drop,
Splash,
The water is falling,
Drip,
Drop,
Splash,
The sky is drooling,
Umbrellas come in many shapes and sizes,
Designing them you can win prizes.

Molly Joan Turrell (10)
Ivydale Primary School, Nunhead

Umbrella

I have a hoop,
It's shaped like a loop.
I have a dress that is blue,
I want a matching shoe.
On my hat I have a flower,
And it is very dour.
When I look down, it is dry,
And when I look up there's lovely sky.

Tyra Lafayette
Ivydale Primary School, Nunhead

Poetry Explorers – South & West London

Love In The Rain

Remember me when I am gone away
Gone far away to a far better place
Never again will we meet face to face
Going to live in another day
Remember me from week to day
Remember the future we planned to make
But now the future has passed away
And also remember the nights we used to pray
If you have to let me go
Just remember our days in the snow
And remember how our love glowed
In a really fast daisy mode
Our love didn't last that long
And for very long I just stayed strong.

Darelle Hernandez (10)
Ivydale Primary School, Nunhead

Umbrella

U p the umbrellas go.
M ight fly away so don't let it go.
B ring your umbrella just in case, you never know!
R ight at the last minute.
E very day it's really gloomy.
L ike a bird doing a loopy.
L ike a footballer going loony.
A lways bring an umbrella.

Tia Briscoe-Alexander (9)
Ivydale Primary School, Nunhead

A Garden

If I should have a garden
I know how it should be
All the different colours
Red, blue, yellow, green
White, purple and orange
A dog would chase a ball
A frog would sit and eat
A little cat would play
With a little piece of string
And in the very middle
I'd only have to stand
For ladybirds and butterflies
To settle on my hand.

Nell Amos (8)
Ivydale Primary School, Nunhead

Questions

Why are people scared of mice?
Why do people tell stories?
Why are people always sad?
Why are dragons always fierce?
Why do frogs always burp?
Why do fires keep me warm?
Why does snow keep me cold?
Why is the Earth always lost, going round in circles?
Why is space so vast?
Why are people always talking?
And why, oh why, am I asking all these questions?

Willard Richards-Gray (8)
Ivydale Primary School, Nunhead

Love In Puddles

Remember me when I am gone away
Gone far away into a new land
Now I can't hold you in the palm of my hand
But please don't remember me in the wrong way!

Remember me day by day
I have a new life
With a new wife
But you will always have a place to stay!

Yet, if you forget me
I will always be in your heart
There will always be a part
I hope you believe me, my ex-wife.

Sade Rasheda Mavoka (10)
Ivydale Primary School, Nunhead

Umbrellas

Sheltering me from the rain,
As it trickles down to the drain,
In the wind the umbrella flies,
Making its way to the sky,

The rain pelts down,
As I walk through the field,
But I won't get soaked,
Because the umbrella's my shield,
The sun is covered by horrid black clouds,
And the thunder and lightning is tremendously loud.

Joe Ward (10)
Ivydale Primary School, Nunhead

Umbrellas

Whenever it rains you need shelter,
An umbrella is like your little helper,
A umbrella blocks out the rain,
Which goes straight into the drain,

Your umbrella is your shield,
And the rain helps things grow in the field,
You can play in the puddles,
When you catch a cold you get lots of cuddles,

When you open your umbrella in your house, you get bad luck,
But when you fall in slushy muck, you turn into a big blob of muck,
When you use your umbrella like Mary Poppins to fly,
You'll be way up high in the sky.

Harriet Arinze (11)
Ivydale Primary School, Nunhead

Snow

Snow comes accidentally day or night,
When it comes, it gives some people a fright,
Why does snow come? Because it's cold,
Snow is never getting old,
When it snows we have to wrap up warm,
People get tired so they yawn,
To me snow is the best weather,
To some people, it's such a bother.

N'Tanya Clark (10)
Ivydale Primary School, Nunhead

Umbrellas

Umbrellas help me to keep dry
Let's just hope mine doesn't fly.
When we see the rain, umbrellas up again,
And we all hope it leaves.
The rain brings forth flowers with all its heavy showers.
But maybe the rain is not such a pain,
Lucky for those little drains.
Finally the rain is gone, happy faces are back
But the ground is still wet.
Everyone waiting for the sun to set
So the umbrellas can start drying.

At least for now . . .

Karen Annang (11)
Ivydale Primary School, Nunhead

Rain!

Rain is a pain,
It drives me insane,
But I love it when I'm in Nunhead Lane.

It falls from the sky,
Goes into the drain,
Down through the sewers,
Drowning the rats out to sea.

Nina Solomon (10)
Ivydale Primary School, Nunhead

King Neptune's Hand

Waves splash along the beach,
a giant hand trying to reach,
feeling, feeling for the land,
but finding only golden sand,
foaming fingers linger, linger,
falling, falling back away,
ready to come back another day.

Max Rampton (9)
Ivydale Primary School, Nunhead

School

S chool can be fun,
C hildren work hard,
H aving fun is what you want,
O ther children just read a book,
O therwise they work,
L iteracy and numeracy can be hard
   But if you work well you'll get a good mark.

Chloe Sweet (10)
Ivydale Primary School, Nunhead

Love Is . . .

Love is good, just like a good cake
Love is fantastic, like Fantastic Mr Fox
Will you ever turn and look me in the eye?
Love is romantic and I would do anything for you
I'm on fire without you
So I'll let you know I love you.
Love is . . .

Layla Chaudhury-Laird (8)
Ivydale Primary School, Nunhead

The Girl On The Streets

I am not tall,
But I have it all.
Look at the sky,
It is as grey as my eye.
All these lies
Are hurting my eyes.

Marie-Louise Beatrice Jugant (9)
Ivydale Primary School, Nunhead

Umbrellas

There once was a man in a cellar,
who liked to sell umbrellas,
one day he sold twenty-four,
which sadly broke the law,
and he ended up a bad fella!

Harry Surey (10)
Ivydale Primary School, Nunhead

Rain

R ain is so mad
A nd most of the time I'm sad
I n the rain I stand
N ever will it stop while I watch the band.

Theodore Jugant (8)
Ivydale Primary School, Nunhead

My Sweet-Bitter Brother

My brother and I always fight,
I am sure he's is wrong
he thinks he's right.

He pinches my toys,
when I am not there.
He cheats at games,
he is never fair.

He leaves his clothes
all over the place.
If I complain, he pulls a face.
Sweet bitter brother.

Every morning I have to wait
to take him to school,
we are always late.

But however naughty he can be,
he is still my brother,
nothing must harm him,
he is smaller than me.
Sweet bitter brother.

Ella Tshibambi-Niles (10)
Kingswood Primary School, Lambeth

School Time

School is fun,
School is cool,

But not when Mr Tunstall steps on that stool,
Maybe he wants to shout at us all.

In literacy, I earned a handwriting pen
In maths my favourite number is ten.

In the playground children skip and trip.
Hula hoop, hula hoop, goes round and round,
some people like me, just drop it onto the ground.

We have assemblies every morning,
it's so boring so I start yawning,
mostly I'm snoring.

I think my friend Blaisie is a little bit crazy
and I think Dylan is quite a villain.

But as I said before, *please* do not ignore . . .

School is fun,
School is cool!

Zara Wilson (8)
Kingswood Primary School, Lambeth

Words

Words that speak,
Words that call,
Words in books,
Words on walls.
Words that are loud,
Words that are quiet,
Words that shout
And make a riot.
Words that move,
Words that crawl,
Words that stand still,
Words that fall.
Words are everywhere,
So beware!

Rasses-Senami Attolou (10)
Kingswood Primary School, Lambeth

The Beach

Waves brushing against the soft, golden sand,
Children playing sandcastles joyfully.
Ice lollies dripping fresh juice.
People surfing among the competitive waves bravely.

The sun shining brightly over the beach.
People smiling gracefully with each other.
People gazing at the beautiful sights.
Seagulls eating the leftovers from fish and chips.
Boys and girls swimming happily in the deep blue sea.

Reann Harrison (11)
Kingswood Primary School, Lambeth

Mum's Ring

I was at home feeling very ecstatic,
I pranced round and round.
I jumped over the chairs and crawled under the tables,
And guess what I had found.

It was my mum's ruby-red ring,
I tried it on for size.
My eyes went in a black and white spiral,
I was then hypnotised.

I looked like a monkey,
And talked like a dog.
I smelled like a skunk,
And hopped like a frog.

Mum found out,
And reversed the spell.
She told me she was a witch,
I just had to . . . *yell!*

Tiffany Ndukwe (11)
Linton Mead Primary School, Thamesmead

Silence Listens

It was so quiet that
I heard the wind sneezing.

It was so quiet that
I heard the door closing.

It was so quiet that
I heard the birds sing outside the window.

Nadia Szoma (9)
Linton Mead Primary School, Thamesmead

Snowflakes

Snowflakes don't look alike,
Snowflakes are really white.

Snowflakes make blankets of snow,
Snowflakes move fast or really slow.

Snowflakes are really small,
Snowflakes fit through the smallest hole.

Snowflakes are really cold,
Don't let them touch you when you're bald.

Snowflakes melt when they touch you,
Snowflakes will never melt you.

Some people like snowflakes,
Some people don't,
I really like snowflakes,
They are the best.

Vlad Miclaus (9)
Linton Mead Primary School, Thamesmead

Respect

R espect
E ach other, we are all
S pecial.
P eople are all the same
E specially teachers and other
C hildren. People need
T o learn to respect.

Nicholas Eker-Moura (8)
Linton Mead Primary School, Thamesmead

Wonderful Linton Mead

Linton Mead is very fine
If the sky is gloomy, we make the sun shine
Linton Mead is very great
Our teachers say it too
We like to fix and create
And we only want to stay at home if we have the flu
Linton Mead is the very best school
You would love it there
Even children say Linton Mead is cool
Because everyone is fair

If you don't believe me
Go and see
Please come to Linton Mead
Don't make me plead.

Fatimah Mohd-Fauzi (8)
Linton Mead Primary School, Thamesmead

Snow

Snow is fun, snow is cool
Snow is the best time of the year.

Snow is cold, snow is the best
I like snow because it is my favourite.

Snow is slippery, snow is freezing.

Snow is cold, so remember to wear
Your hat, scarf, gloves and jacket.

Nathaniel Olalekan (9)
Linton Mead Primary School, Thamesmead

Snow, Snow

Snow, snow, you glow so bright,
Snow, snow, you're so high.

Snow, snow, you come in winter,
Snow, snow, you're as white as a printer.

Why didn't you fall in December or January?
But you came instead in February.

The snow angels fly about,
But soon they'll lie about.

Snow, snow, you shine like a crystal,
Snow, snow, you're bigger than a pistol.

Snow, snow, time to go,
Bye snow, time to go.

Ore Akin-Odidi (10)
Linton Mead Primary School, Thamesmead

The Tree

The tree is as big as an elephant.
The tree's leaves are as green as grass.
The green leaves go through with the wind.
Sometimes the bees go around the tree.
The branches of the tree are as hard as a brick.
There are even bright and light apples on the tree.
No one will knock down the tree because sometimes there are bees.

Abayomi Olawale Lawal (9)
Linton Mead Primary School, Thamesmead

Planet Earth/People

This is the western world
Full of money and fear
With all the fine facilities
There is no humanity to bear.

I am fed up of people
Trying to be fit
They always waste food
And try to be rich.

Many children are spoiled
With all the new things
They don't appreciate anything
Not even what luck brings.

Habeeb Periklis Lawal (9)
Linton Mead Primary School, Thamesmead

Brown

Brown is the colour of tree bark,
Brown is the colour of someone's hair,
Brown is the colour of a pheasant's feather.

Brown is popular, brown is cool,
But brown is my skin colour, dude!

Brown is the colour of twigs,
Brown is the colour of my jumper,
Brown is the colour of my bike,
Brown is the colour that I like.

Brown is the colour that shows I'm honourable.

Oreoluwa Ola Kareem (10)
Linton Mead Primary School, Thamesmead

Fire

I can be blazing hot
And easily burn a pot.
My colour can be fiery red
And I can burn your head.
In a flash
You can be turned into ash.
I spread as quickly as a disease
I am more than a swarm of bees.
I can be orange and yellow
And be used to roast marshmallows.
Sometimes I am blue
And I will not give you another clue.

Siti Nur Syakirah Mohd-Fauzi (10)
Linton Mead Primary School, Thamesmead

Aliyah Miah

A liyah is my name
L ove is in my heart
I always like to share
Y ou will always find a smile on my face
A lways helping my friends out
H aving fun is my game.

M y two sisters are a pain but
I still love them anyway.
A lways trying hard in class to
H ave good marks, to be the best.

Aliyah Miah (7)
Linton Mead Primary School, Thamesmead

Dancing

D azzling dancer twirling and spinning
A mazing actor and singer
N ow it is my time to shine
C hirpy and cheerful, cheering out loud
I rresistibly fantastic
N ever-ending twirling
G liding gracefully across the gleaming floor.

Chloe Kiernan (9)
Linton Mead Primary School, Thamesmead

Fola's Friend Rap

I was playing with my ball
I saw this child, he was so small
We had a little chat, made friends and went to the mall
He had an accident and fell off a wall
He got up and went to the hall
He wanted to call all
To come to play with his ball.

Folarin Aina (9)
Linton Mead Primary School, Thamesmead

Poetry Explorers — South & West London

Haikus

The brain in my head
Struggles to think of ideas
And I am anxious.

The toes on my feet
Tired of walking around
When we're out shopping.

Amy Elizabeth Honour & Deborah Afolabi (9)
Linton Mead Primary School, Thamesmead

Hannah

H appy
A dorable
N ever naughty
N ice
A ngelic
H ard worker.

Hannah Jones (8)
Linton Mead Primary School, Thamesmead

Tigers

T igers are one of the most
I ndestructible animals in the
G alaxy and on
E arth, they can also
R oar loudly, they are very
S trong.

Kelvin Ihama (8)
Linton Mead Primary School, Thamesmead

Oyinda

O range is my third favourite colour.
Y ellow is a bright colour.
I taly is my best friend's country.
N elly is my friend and she shouts.
D ogs are not nice, I say.
A nd I am special and OK?

Oyindamola Adelaiye (8)
Linton Mead Primary School, Thamesmead

Happiness

Happiness is clear like a window.
It tastes like fish fingers.
It smells like a fresh wind.
It looks like children playing.
It sounds like my nieces talking to me.
It feels like I'm asleep.

Sacha Waite (8)
Linton Mead Primary School, Thamesmead

Poetry

P oetry
O ther people respect it
E veryone likes it
T eachers love it
R espect your work
Y oung people.

Lois Ann Moore (8)
Linton Mead Primary School, Thamesmead

Stars

S tars shimmer like a rose fainting,
T winkle like a diamond painting.
A mazing gorgeous stars in my sight,
R ight star is the brightest star in the night.
S ome are so kind they have little diamonds in the middle.

Oyindamola Onasanya (8)
Linton Mead Primary School, Thamesmead

Poppy

P oppy is
O bviously
P retty and
P olite, also
Y oung.

Poppy Howes (8)
Linton Mead Primary School, Thamesmead

Sasha

S asha is
A bonny girl
S he loves
H er family
A nd school.

Sasha Roots (8)
Linton Mead Primary School, Thamesmead

Poetry Explorers – South & West London

The Girl Who Wore Black

There once was a girl who wore black,
She thought it would bring her brain back,
She went out in the night,
And thought it was too bright.
How sad was the girl who wore black.

Michelle Ndukwe (9)
Linton Mead Primary School, Thamesmead

My Fruit Is A Plum

My fruit is juicy
My fruit is purple
My fruit is sweet
My fruit's a plum.

Laura Umoh (7)
Linton Mead Primary School, Thamesmead

Star

S himmering in the night sky,
T wisting and turning, never ever stopping,
A t the end of night, dawn rises consuming the night sky,
R ecreating a new day.

Jason Poon (9)
Linton Mead Primary School, Thamesmead

Liam

L iam is good at school
I 'm very smart
A t
M aths.

Liam Dand (8)
Linton Mead Primary School, Thamesmead

The Snow Keeps Falling

Cosy warm houses,
People huddling by blazing fires,
Snuggling up under duvets,
And the snow keeps falling.

Cars skidding and sliding on dangerous roads,
No work, no school,
Streets are deserted,
And the snow keeps falling.

Children playing joyfully,
Sledging down hills,
Throwing snowballs with frozen hands,
And the snow keeps falling.

Snow is like a white blanket on the ground,
Snowflakes plunging towards you like a swarm of bees,
Snowballs sailing through the air elegantly,
And the snow keeps falling.

Snowball fights in the ice-cold park,
Snowmen grinning like meerkats,
People carving snow sculptures and igloos,
And the snow keeps falling.

Everyone is desperate for hot drinks,
Bustling cafes are bursting with customers,
Children doodling on steamy windows,
And the snow keeps falling.

Weather warms up,
Snowflakes fade away, snowmen melt,
The snowy fun has finished,
Spring is on the way!

Jennie Connelly (9)
Little Ealing Primary School, Ealing

Favourite Foods

You can get it crunchy or smooth,
Get it in sandwiches and it will ooze,
Some people like it, some people not,
Some people will just like it a lot.

It is hard as a rock,
It is liked by many,
As tasty as sweets,
As brown as mud.

Get them big and small,
All different flavours,
You get them crunchy,
They are skinny but tasty.

Cold as ice,
All different tastes,
With chocolate flakes,
With crispy cones.

Peanut butter,
Chocolate,
Crisps,
Ice cream.

Jennie Connelly & Carys Hindry (9)
Little Ealing Primary School, Ealing

Fabulous Summer Days

Summer, fabulous days,
Always send me away.
There's a slight breeze
Near the summer trees.

I lose my sight,
Today it is bright,
In the sun,
I need a bun.

I have seen all my friends
And the day is about to end,
My maid is a fool,
And I'm really cool.

I feel hot,
Quite a lot.
I have a mate called Jed,
And he has a cute ted.

I feel in the mood,
For some tasty hot food,
I need a drink,
I'll get it out of the sink.

Maiya Harrison-Genis (8)
Little Ealing Primary School, Ealing

Rain

Rain is softly falling,
It is freezing and wet,
Rain, it is getting cloudy
And grey.

It is beating down,
When it lands on plants and bushes,
It smells fresh,
At the moment it is like an army falling into battle.

I am drenched, soaked,
It is like a cloud is weeping,
Millions of tears plopping.
Splash! Is all I can hear.

The rain is bucketing down,
As quick as lightning,
It is pouring down,
Like tiny bullets speeding.

The salty rainwater is cold and wet,
Like the sea, dripping endlessly.
It is extremely damp,
Horrible weather!

I feel sad and I am shivering,
I wish the beautiful sun
Would come out, wait . . .
What is that piercing light shining?

It is an incredible rainbow,
As beautiful as the new day.
The wonderful rainbow colour glistens in the puddles.
It might be a glorious day today!

Ravi Dhillon (9)
North Ealing Primary School, Ealing

I Am Autumn

I am autumn,
Full of surprises,
Big and small.

Leaves golden and brown,
Falling on the ground,
Covering green grass.

Fleet of birds,
Under the grey clouds,
Searching for sunlight.

The gusty wind blows,
Twisting and twirling,
Sending leaves down to the ground.

Drying flowers, drooping down,
Making patterns
On the ground.

I am autumn,
Full of surprises,
Big and small.

Anishaa Pattani (8)
North Ealing Primary School, Ealing

The Wild Cat

The wild cat
Is a creature that
Comes out day and night
He is aware
Of creatures that scare
The people passing by.

The wild cat's owner
He is called Omar
He always strikes a pose
With his new clothes.

He has green eyes
He doesn't eat pies
The cat is fat
And he is black.

At the end of his nap
He goes for a *snack!*

Deena Ahmed (9)
North Ealing Primary School, Ealing

Spring

Once upon a spring day
The lovely sunshine in May
It makes the flowers pop up bright
I look and stare at the beautiful sight
Now you know what spring is like
Look around and see the light.

Jago Di Piro (9)
North Ealing Primary School, Ealing

Trixie, The Cat

She looks like a stripy zebra
She has green and yellow eyes like a marble
Her paws are as dark as coal
But her belly is white as snow.

She always purrs in the early morning
She likes to play with her red ball
But chasing birds is her favourite
Her favourite place to sleep is her warm basket.

When you shake her bowl she jumps for her food
But when you give her Catnip, she goes wild
She whizzes round the room like a cheetah
After all the excitement she sleeps like a baby.

Chloe Kenway (8)
North Ealing Primary School, Ealing

I Wish . . .

I wish I could be a dragonfly
and hover like a miniature helicopter
Across the school pond.

I wish I could wear a snail's shell
to protect me from angry words.

I wish I could be the moment
when a laugh takes root
and blossoms in your mouth
and I'd stay there forever,
trapped in that moment of light.

Shougo Kimuna (9)
North Ealing Primary School, Ealing

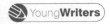

The Chameleon

The chameleon is as slow as a snail.
It is as beautiful as a hummingbird.
It is as still as a statue.
The chameleon is camouflaged to look like a tree.
Suddenly it catches a fly
and eats it up before it can die.
The chameleon sleeps at night
and wakes up when the day is bright.

A Komodo dragon was sleeping under a tree.
The chameleon woke up and said, 'You can't eat me!'
The dragon yawned and said, 'I just might!'
And swallowed the chameleon in one bite!

Kai Wing
North Ealing Primary School, Ealing

Ill

When I'm ill I feel miserable.
There's a rumble in my tummy.
An annoying pain is in my brain.
When I'm ill I feel miserable.

When I'm ill I feel glum.
Quiet things make monstrous noises.
Sounds keep going round and round.
When I'm ill I feel glum.

Freya Gann (8)
North Ealing Primary School, Ealing

The Legend Of A Big Monster

Autumn leaves are falling, now look, behold,
Birds are flying away now, it is getting cold.

I am not allowed out now, my mum is worried,
No one is out on the streets now, everyone has scurried.

It is not to be spoken of, or to be mentioned,
The legend

Of the big monster.

Abigail Bean (8)
North Ealing Primary School, Ealing

Water

Water, water everywhere.
Water, water up in the air.
Water, water in the sea
Crashing and splashing over me.
Water, water in the pond,
Just perfect for the ducks to swim upon.
Water, water good to drink
Water, water helps me think.

James Bartle (9)
North Ealing Primary School, Ealing

Water, Water,

Water, water supports all life,
Water, water turns to ice.
Water, water makes the sea,
Water, water sinks the ships.
Water, water, you can be so smooth and slick.
Water, water covers 70% of the Earth.
Water, water, you sparkle like glitter.
Water, water, we couldn't swim without you.

Matthew Hughes (9)
North Ealing Primary School, Ealing

Chickens

C lucking wildly,
H oused in a coop,
I love to hold them,
C lutching them tight,
K eep them safe,
E ggs just laid, feeling warm,
N o foxes are allowed,
S o safe in the night.

Lucy Henfield (9)
North Ealing Primary School, Ealing

Rabbits

R unning rabbits
A re having a race
B aby bunnies jump and hop
B aby bunnies never stop
I ntelligent bunnies in the hutch
T aking carrots, *munch, munch, munch*
S till running round the hutch, they never tire
    but sometimes when they stop, they look sadly through the wire.

Maisie Backshall (8)
North Ealing Primary School, Ealing

My Birthday

Because it's my birthday
I'm very excited!
Rolls filled with Nutella!
Toys and cards delivered to my house!
Hope I get some Gogos!
Dancing to my favourite songs!
A special day just for me!
Yippee! My favourite day!

Zak Lyons (9)
North Ealing Primary School, Ealing

Snow

Pearly, puffy, powdery snow,
Shine a light on it,
And it starts to glow.

Crystal, crispy, crunchy cotton,
Put on your scarf, hat and mittens.

Make snow angels and snowmen
The fun of snow never ends.

Ranil West
North Ealing Primary School, Ealing

Animals

A is for antelope standing tall and strong.
N is for newt, all slimy and long.
I is for iguana basking in the sun.
M is for monkey having lots of fun.
A is for ant crawling along the ground.
L is for lion making a roaring sound.
S is for snake slithering around.

James Cogan-Tucker (8)
North Ealing Primary School, Ealing

Animals

Big animals, small animals, any size at all animals.
Wild, domesticated and even farm animals.
Large and tiny, fluffy and scaly, but I still love them all.
Forgetful elephants, speedy cheetahs and don't forget the anteaters.
Cats and dogs, birds and fish, rabbits, hamsters and guinea pigs.
Cows and sheep, horses and pigs, chickens and ducks,
Who love to play in the muck!

Kiara Lorenzo (8)
North Ealing Primary School, Ealing

The Final Match

On the 31st of May I went to see the final match of the day
At the stadium there were people everywhere
All excited, cheering and shouting in the air.
The players came on the pitch
One team in blue, one team in red
The first goal was scored by Ronaldo's head
The losing team tried their best, putting all their efforts into the test.

Parsa Sarkis (9)
North Ealing Primary School, Ealing

The Big Crash

'Twas Hallowe'en night, Jane had a bag of sweets.
She was with her friends saying her 'Trick or treats?'
When she reached a woman's house, she knocked on the door.
She looked away, then heard a big crash on the floor!
The door was opened, they saw a vase was smashed,
Her dog knocked it over - that's what crashed!

Lucy Bagot (10)
North Ealing Primary School, Ealing

Earth

In the black velvet sky the stars shone
as bright as diamonds.
The Earth was so still that not even the wind
could make something move.
A shooting star came by, like a meteor.

Romain Potier (9)
North Ealing Primary School, Ealing

Poetry Explorers – South & West London

Animals

There are lots of different animals living in our world.
There's the cheeky monkey and the laughing hyena.
My favourites are the dangerous shark and the fierce lion.
I don't like the stripy zebra or the massive elephant.

Finn Byrne (8)
North Ealing Primary School, Ealing

The Land Of the Shadows

Out of the light and into the dark,
Where many people have ventured,
A burning candle snuffed
By the foul poison of fate.

The land of the shadows that is death.

Out of the light and into the dark,
Leaving the scattered remains
Of mourning family and friends,
Trailing behind as you drift off into the void.

The land of the shadows that is death.

Out of the light and into the dark,
The endless emptiness of space,
Awaiting silently is the land of the shadows,
A new chapter of the book entitled your name.

The land of the shadows that is death.

Thomas Long (10)
Peter Hills School, Rotherhithe

Walking Through The Seasons . . .

Here and now is a time to be glad,
A far-stretching, clear, blue sky, you just can't be sad.
The dew from the grass, as new as can be,
A wonderfully, rare, gold delicacy.
Spring is the first stop to wonder . . .

A golden sun that outshines all around,
Nowhere on Earth can dark be found.
Birds twittering, a sound to behold,
Playing down our road, that never gets old.
Summer, the second stop to Paradise . . .

And then, as if by magic, the green trees turn to brown,
The sound of crunching leaves, it's impossible to frown.
A cool autumn breeze is like Heaven on my face,
Such a wondrous gift to the human race.
Autumn is the third stop to great feelings . . .

Then, with one, great flash, the land is covered in white
A *huge* crystal blanket, a superb sight.
Happy times and many days off school,
And Christmas, deep inside of it all,
Winter, one step away from glory, this is true!

But the best thing, I tell you, now it's quite plain,
Is that all of these things start all over again . . .

Sam Brooks-Martin (10)
Peter Hills School, Rotherhithe

Poetry Explorers — South & West London

My Horniman Museum Trip

H istory is in this museum,
O nly the best,
R eally interesting and fun,
N othing can ever bring it down,
I nteresting facts,
M ums, dads . . . everyone can come,
A beautiful place to do some research,
N ow or later you *must* come!

M ountains of fun for everyone,
U nderwater animals,
S o come on down and have a nosy around,
E xciting and
U nique,
M ovie night . . . forget it, let's go to the
                        Horniman Museum!

Khamille Gordon (9)
Peter Hills School, Rotherhithe

If Children Ruled The World!

If children ruled the world
Maths would be banned
Mums would have to go to work.
Children would have all the money across the land.

My birthday is in December
I just wish it were in May for one day.
So come on children everywhere.
It's time to get our way.

Rebecca Evans
Peter Hills School, Rotherhithe

Horniman Museum

It
was great
so, so cool
the best trip ever
learnt it all
I'll go
again
to
have fun
again and again
I travelled so far
but yes,
it was
worth
it.

Brooke Morgan (9)
Peter Hills School, Rotherhithe

If Children Ruled The World

If children ruled the world
We could play with glitter,
Just have fun
Oranges will get bitter.

Play around
Go to the loo,
It's time
Let's watch 'Doctor Who'!

Remy Soares (9)
Peter Hills School, Rotherhithe

Horniman Museum!

H elp from the people,
O bjects are interesting,
R elatives can come too,
N early the best sweets in the shop,
I nstruments are cool.
M ummies from history,
A ll the fish in the aquarium,
N othing is ever boring.

M usic from other countries,
U nexpected animals,
S eeing things alive,
E veryone is kind,
U ndoubtedly you will love it,
M eant for everyone.

Bobbi Tassell (10)
Peter Hills School, Rotherhithe

If Children Ruled The World

If children ruled the world
maths would be banned
and adults sent to university
right on the sand.

My birthday is in February
could it ever be in May?
So come on children everywhere
it's time to get our way.

Carlotta Falsetti-Flatt (8)
Peter Hills School, Rotherhithe

If Children Ruled The World

If children ruled the world
pollution would be banned
children would go to bed at twelve
all across the land.

Everyone would be nice, children too.
children would have fun,
adults would be sent to a building site
and have to carry a tonne.

So come on children,
run, jump and play,
let's rule the world
let's get our way!

Maddison Clancy (8)
Peter Hills School, Rotherhithe

If Children Ruled The World

If children ruled the world,
Vegetables would be banned,
Sweet shops would be open
Throughout the land.

Weekends will be sunny,
I will have a laugh,
If I can't stop the wars,
You won't have a bath.

Ayomide Dina (9)
Peter Hills School, Rotherhithe

Horniman

H ooray for Horniman
O pen all the time
R eady with loads of fun
N eeded all the time
I ncredible fish inside their aquarium
M ost best museum in the world
A magical place full of wonders
N ever leave bored.

Jamie Smith (9)
Peter Hills School, Rotherhithe

Horniman

H orniman Museum was a lot of fun
O ur class was well-behaved with a few mums
R eading and looking at lots of fish
N o one was bored but some children I did miss
I t was all really interesting, reading all about the animals
M any people were looking at camels
A t once the teachers told us to go back to our place
N ow we had to go home but at least we made it safe.

Ajay Fadeyi (10)
Peter Hills School, Rotherhithe

Horniman

H ad a fantastic time
O pen to everybody
R emember what instruments you liked
N ice day it was at the Horniman
I nteresting facts we found
M aking noises with the drum
A magical place, full of wonders for use.
N ever say you are bored there.

Monique Brodie-Mends (10)
Peter Hills School, Rotherhithe

Horniman

H as lots to see
O bjects so fantastic
R ight in this building
N atural history
I s really fascinating
M ummies from years ago
A nd loads more
N othing to regret seeing.

Ellie Segar (9)
Peter Hills School, Rotherhithe

Outer Space

I'm on a space mission,
What a great expedition!
I'm walking on the moon,
Like a loon.

I'm jumping from star to star,
Like I'm in a car.
I'm orbiting the Earth,
It's really fun you know.
I've landed on the moon,
Its face as white as snow.

Queuing for the rocket
Isn't as fun as it looks,
That's why I've brought some reading books.
When you're on the rocket,
It's very boring,
From here I can hear the great, big engine roaring.

People back home hope that we are safe,
But we don't care as long as we're in our lair,
That's all that matters.

We've landed safe at home,
All I've left on the moon,
Is my pottery gnome.
I will remember and treasure this day,
Because it felt like Santa's wide, open sleigh.

Edward Paterson (8)
Robin Hood Primary School, Kingston Vale

What Red Means To Me

Red, oh red,
What is it to me?
The bright red sunset
That shines down on thee.

In summer, the flower I see so fine,
Is the rose that is as red as wine.

Red is for danger,
So beware!
For the red flame of fire,
You must take care.

Also in anger, the colour you see
Is someone's red face looking at me!

Lauren Sheree Edwards (8)
Robin Hood Primary School, Kingston Vale

The Sun And The Moon

One day when I woke up
I saw the sun and the moon,
That day was the funniest day,
Every day I'd seen nothing but gloomy days

Today the flowers were blooming,
And the trees dancing,
Everything was funny, I really liked it,
So I said to God,
'Can it be like this every day?'

Tharushi S Bhagya Denipitiya (8)
Robin Hood Primary School, Kingston Vale

Florida Life

My first time in Florida
was great fun you see
it just kept getting jollier
the more that I would see.

I got up every morning
and jumped into the pool
I would hear my daddy snoring
and watch my brother acting cool.

Sometimes we played mini golf
I didn't always win!
I tried to win by crying 'wolf''
and knocking the golf ball in!

Emma Hall (8)
Robin Hood Primary School, Kingston Vale

The Sun And The Moon

The sun is rising,
The moon is resting,
All day through.
It comes out at night,
Just to see you.
The moon is out,
The sun is about,
To wake up soon.
The moon will go
In the afternoon.
While it's night-time,
Birds sing their songs.
After a while,
They sing songs all day long.

Renée Osaze Eguavoen (9)
St Anne's RC Primary School, Vauxhall

Skiing The Mountain

Shooting down the run, dodging all the bumps,
Trying to keep my eyes open for all the super jumps.
Avoiding amateur skiers, who just get in my way,
If I'm not careful, there'll be a price to pay.
Bombing down the run, not worrying that I'll fall,
The only thought in my head is trying to look cool.
Looking for a challenge, something new to try,
Then the miraculous white mountains suddenly catch my eye.
Looking down on the snow, reflecting the shining sun,
What a wonderful piece of work our magnificent God has done.

Milo Rose (10)
St Benedict's Junior School, Ealing

My Brothers

One is tall and lean,
Thinks he's a babe machine,
Flexes his guns,
Whilst eating buns,
Always playing rugby,
Always smelly and grubby!

Number two - loves to pose,
Modelling new clothes,
Nothing is ever his fault,
Even when he's caught,
He sings and drums,
Which annoys us some.

They both annoy me,
Fight and tease me,
They think they are smarter,
Just cos they are faster,
Having brothers is no treat,
Two of the ugliest you could meet.

Two for sale!
Do you want them?

Bethany Porter (9)
St Benedict's Junior School, Ealing

Teachers

Making flipcharts
Making worksheets
Making us work!

Finding fun web sites
Finding website challenges
Finding time to develop us!

Don't believe in excuses
Don't allow us to make noises
Don't allow us to let ourselves down!

Sending us to detentions
Sending us to the headmaster
Sending us to progress ourselves!

Strict but fair!
Hard but encouraging!
Disciplining us but letting us have fun!

Thank you for being there for us!

Alvin Lee (10)
St Benedict's Junior School, Ealing

Seasons

Summer is a warm season
Winter is so cold
Autumn is a leafy season
Spring is so bouncy
I love all the seasons
And I have given you all the reasons.

Philip Byrnes (7)
St Benedict's Junior School, Ealing

Poetry Explorers – South & West London

The Cow

Milk creamy
Cowpat steamy
Hide leather
Not clever
Slow walker
Non talker
Chews the cud
Loves the mud
Hair slick
Cows lick
Beefy meat
Tasty treat
Brown eyes
Tail flies
Lifetime pass
To eat grass.
The cow.

Shane Duffy (8)
St Benedict's Junior School, Ealing

Winter's Wonders

The freshening breeze, *zzzz* . . .
The rustling leaves, so crispy . . .
Birds' wings, glistening in the sun
The moistured grass being trampled by feet . . .
The trees are dying of age, trying to hang onto life

These are winter's wonders.

Edward Sullivan (9)
St Benedict's Junior School, Ealing

David Beckham

D avid Beckham plays football in America,
A long with his wife and all of their sons.
V ictoria is very skinny, I think she has gone off buns.
I n 1992, Beckham played professional footie for Man U.
D avid Beckham has played over one hundred games, how many
    more can he do?
B eckham has had six hairstyles in his career and he has been
    known for them.
E veryone knows who he is and likes him.
C ruz, Romeo and Brooklyn are the names of Beckham's offspring.
K icking a football into goal is Beckham's favourite thing.
H ow LA Galaxy bought Beckham for one million dollars,
    I don't know.
A C Milan want to sign a contract for Beckham, they won't be shy!
M ilan say they are desperate for him, I'm sure they will
    manage to buy.

Casimir Bowyer (11)
St Benedict's Junior School, Ealing

Car

Fast mover
All colours
Strong puller
Land Rover
Metal monster
All sizer

Car.

Thomas Zussman (8)
St Benedict's Junior School, Ealing

Poetry Explorers — South & West London

July

July - you are a happy boy
On the bright, sandy beach.
You are a time for fun,
No time to teach.
A bright blue bucket and
A blazing red spade,
You show off with pride
The castles you've made.

Eating a cool ice cream,
A beam of sun on your face,
You splash in the shimmering water,
Swimming with grace.
Long, lazy evenings
You play with your friends.
Oh, July,
I wish you would never end!

Finn Hobson (10)
St Benedict's Junior School, Ealing

Wriggly Worm

The wriggly, wiggly worm
It always squirms
It twists and turns
Until
It is time to learn

Oh that wriggly, wiggly worm
How he always squirms.

Cristina Moran (9)
St Benedict's Junior School, Ealing

Glory Be To God

Glory is to God for the amazing trees,
The crackle of burning fire on coal.
Thank you for the thunder that flashes and bangs
And the waves that smash and crash.
Thank you for the setting sun on the beautiful horizon
And the birds that sing in the sunrise.

Thank you for the beautiful turquoise sea
And the multicoloured fish.
Thank you for all the animals that slither in the sunlight
And the crashing waterfall and the trickling over stones,
The beautiful stars shining in the shimmering darkness.
Thank you for the sparkling snow.
Praise Him,
Amen!

Hector Hardman (10)
St Benedict's Junior School, Ealing

Pancake Day

It's pancake day, I say, *'Hip hip hooray!'*
Flour, eggs, milk, whisk it until it's smooth as silk.
Get the frying pan and make it hot,
Pour in the mixture and cook the lot.

Round like the sun, my pancake is cooked.
Lemons and sugar I have shook.
Into my tummy and it's very yummy.
I love pancakes.
Hip hip hooray!

Gabriel Kerr (8)
St Benedict's Junior School, Ealing

Richard Hammond

R ichard Hammond is
I n a show, along with Jezza and
C aptain Slow.
H e really likes racing
A nd will do it any day.
R ichard loves his Porsche but he
D oesn't like James May.

H amster to his fans
A nd also to his mates.
M ost other nicknames he just hates.
M any think he's the best,
O thers think he's just a pest.
N obody could disagree,
D riving's a sport loved by he!

Dominic King (11)
St Benedict's Junior School, Ealing

A Gorilla

Big and fat
Strong as an ox
Hands as big as boxing gloves
Fierce as a tiger
Brave as a lion
Black as the night
But the teeth are white
Like a lion, strong as iron.

A gorilla.

Stefain Serkilar (8)
St Benedict's Junior School, Ealing

Tiger Shark

As fast as lightning
Rubbish eater
Bloodthirsty
Blood maker

So big, so fighting
Fish chaser
Man-hungry
Man hater

As silent as a dream
Sonic smeller
Ocean beauty
Deep thinker

One angry, tiger shark!

Tobias Campbell (9)
St Benedict's Junior School, Ealing

Summer

Summer is the sun shining in my face.
It's flying, flapping birds in Heaven.
Summer is like a funny joke.
Summer is an apple on a tree.
It has no limits and no beginning.
It's a bunch of apples jumping in the sun.
Summer has wings of gold and silver.
Summer is a time for fun and play.
Summer is the best.

Luke Cassidy (9)
St Benedict's Junior School, Ealing

Poetry Explorers – South & West London

I Don't Cry

Throat burns,
Eyes sting,
Face swells,
Frightening.

Nose sniffs,
Lips quake,
Chin trembles,
Legs shake.

Tears drop.

You what?
Crying?
Me! Cry?
Nah - I've just got something in my eye . . .

Katherine Reid (10)
St Benedict's Junior School, Ealing

Hamster

Hamster, shaking his bed,
Tapping his water bottle,
Crunching his food,
Rustling his straw,
Nibbling the bars to his cage,
That's
Him,
My
Hamster!

Alexander Hughes (9)
St Benedict's Junior School, Ealing

The Dog

Attention seeker
Day waster
Bum sniffer
Sun lazer
Cat chaser
Mouse eater
Flea carrier
Wolf howler
Meat taker
Territory marker
Water shaker
Walk needer

Dog

Edward Hansell (8)
St Benedict's Junior School, Ealing

A Cheetah

Swift runner
Deer gobbler
Good hunter
Spotty prowler
Catty stalker
Tree climber
Teeth sharpener
Furry eater
Clawed killer.

A cheetah.

Patrick Edis (9)
St Benedict's Junior School, Ealing

Pig

Mud lover
Scrap eater
Smell creator
Fat grower
Oink maker
Dribble shedder
Pink skinner
Hairy backer
Trotter footed
Snout nosed
Big space user
Curly tailer

Pig.

Joss Bell (9)
St Benedict's Junior School, Ealing

A Dog

Cat chaser
   Squirrel hunter
      Meat eater
         Chicken lover
            Happy cuddler
               Tail wagger
                  Chatty barker
                     Ball pouncer
                        People befriender.

A dog.

Madeleine Harris (8)
St Benedict's Junior School, Ealing

Legoland

Legoland full with Lego
Giant Lego characters standing next to you,
It is filled with Lego wonders,
If you shrink and go to something Lego,
You will be in Legoland,
Think of all the fun you can have,
Playing with Lego man,
Going through the Lego,
You can explore the deep dangers,
Legoland, Legoland,
It is really fun,
There is nothing better than Legoland,
So you should go there one day.

Eddie Szlachetko (8)
St Benedict's Junior School, Ealing

Fox

Chicken snatcher
Rabbit eater
Silent creeper
Master plotter
Fast runner
Farmer hater
Waste consumer
Good hearer
Brilliant hunter

Fox.

Lorcan O'Brien (9)
St Benedict's Junior School, Ealing

Schools

If you go to a normal school,
It seems to be quite fun,
You will never be bored,
And your teachers are number one.

You can go to any school,
They are all the same,
There's no fault about your school,
There's no one you blame.

You will get really smart,
You will get really clever,
You will feel happier
And you will keep this feeling forever.

Robert Drepaul (8)
St Benedict's Junior School, Ealing

Australia, Australia, I Love You

I love Australia, it is where my family lives.
Whenever I think of it, I have a smile upon my face
And my heart begins to race.
The sky is always blue.
Australia, Australia, I love you!

The sand is a golden yellow.
The sea is crystal clear.
I try to hold the memories in my head
Until I return next year.
Australia, Australia, *I love you!*

Isabella Wingrave (9)
St Benedict's Junior School, Ealing

A Rugby Poem

Today we had a rugby match
Our team was playing away
We jumped into the minibus
And sang all the way.

When we got there
We didn't know what to do
So Mr Knights said, 'Go over
And take off your shoes.'

We dressed into the rest of our kit
We went on the pitch (half an hour later)
Daniel scored the winning try
And I said, 'You are the GI!'

Jordan Bedeau (10)
St Benedict's Junior School, Ealing

Mummy

Dog lover
Good chatter
Not fatter
Hug giver
Sun bather
Wine drinker
Fashion diva
Excellent painter
Jewellery maker

Best mother.

George Charlesworth (8)
St Benedict's Junior School, Ealing

My Cousin

My cousin is a cheeky monkey.
A 24/7 joker.
The maths lesson you have on Monday morning.
A speeding bullet.
A lightning strike.
The chirpy robin in the tree.
A comedian on the telly.
A gentle giant.
The bouncy round chair.
A grand white house.
A very impatient dog.

But I like my cousin really!

Rachel de Cintra (9)
St Benedict's Junior School, Ealing

The Night Sky

The stars shoot through the sky,
And the moon shines right in my eye.

When you're asleep, the room is dark,
There is nothing to see until the sunlight appears.

While you're asleep the foxes come out,
The eagles fly down to muck about.

All these things go into your head,
And lovely dreams happen while you're in your bed.

There is no one about and all is quiet,
Except the foxes fighting about.

Thomas Goode (8)
St Benedict's Junior School, Ealing

September

September is a blow
On your cheeks,
The sun shines
Like a summer's day,
He wears shorts and
T-shirts and goes
Punting on the river,
Picnics are his thing,
Having fun in the sun,
September smiles as
The cold wintry wind
Blows it away.

Sam Loveless (11)
St Benedict's Junior School, Ealing

Robot

I knew a little robot
He said his name was Ted
One day he lost his neck screw
And that blew off his head
I went into a screw shop
To see if there was one more
But I could not find another
And that was just a bore
So now my little robot
Is nicknamed 'Headless Ted'
Because he lost his neck screw
And that blew off his head.

Christopher Pullen (10)
St Benedict's Junior School, Ealing

My Twin Brother

My name is Liam
My twin brother's called Jack
If I say something is white, he will say it is black!
We never agree on the things we like
For example, he likes to drive and I like to bike.

I have brown eyes and he has blue
I love Arsenal and he loves Man U

We are not identical but we both are smart
That's why teachers can't tell us apart
But at the end of the day, it's plain to see
That my brother Jack will always be a part of me!

Liam Carty-Howe (9)
St Benedict's Junior School, Ealing

Spider-Man

Web spinner
Crime fighter
City protector
World saver
New York hero
Spider bitten
Building swinger
High flier
Urban avenger
Metropolis lookout.

Spider-Man.

Tristan Jenkin-Gomez (9)
St Benedict's Junior School, Ealing

Henry VIII

Sword thruster
Battle winner
Clever charmer
Sly liar
Wife wedder
Wife beheader
Big eater
Fat plumper
Long reigner
Mad ruler.
Henry VIII.

Lewis Cox (9)
St Benedict's Junior School, Ealing

The Secret Of The Fish

I sneak up on tadpoles.
I swim with frogs.
I watch children play.
I'll sneak up on you.
I'm a fish.
I swim slowly as a snail,
Or as fast as a shark.
I'll zigzag or swish,
You'll never know the secret
Of the fish.

Ellie Scott (10)
St Benedict's Junior School, Ealing

Night

Night is a murderer moving towards his prey,
His spiky red hair as red as a rose.
His eyes like a black hole with fire inside,
His dark robes floating above the ground,
He silently climbs up the stairs, plunging them into darkness.
He silently jumps onto my bed,
He stabs me with nightmares!
He screams!
The sun has stabbed him with light,
And he dies!

Sam Lubkowski (10)
St Benedict's Junior School, Ealing

Tiger Shark

Aggressive ripper,
A deep swimmer,
A terrifying predator,
A dashing mover,
A rubbish eater,
A grey striped tiger.

What is my animal?

Tiger shark.

James Worrall (8)
St Benedict's Junior School, Ealing

A Teacher

Child's nightmare
Everybody's dread
Hot-tempered one
Demerit giver
Naughty boy catcher
House point giver
Good educator.

A teacher.

Charles Ayson Parrish (9)
St Benedict's Junior School, Ealing

Cow

Super pooper,
Grass eater,
Milk maker,
Weather forecaster,
Mega mooer,
Long chewer,
Beef giver,

Cow.

Luke Rutherford (8)
St Benedict's Junior School, Ealing

William Taylor

He's Usain Bolt waiting to run.
He's our version of Jason Robinson scoring a try.
He's fearless, he's kind, he's our gentle giant.
He's a time bomb in a fish bowl.
He's an explosion on the field.
He's a friend like nothing else.
He's the only William Taylor.

Freddie Greenwood (9)
St Benedict's Junior School, Ealing

The Zoo

Living in the zoo we are bored.
Being locked up in a cage we are sad and upset.
There is no freedom in the zoo.
There is no space in our cramped cages.
There is no peace in the zoo,
With children screaming, adults shouting,
And rude people staring at us all day.

Theodore Hyams (8)
St Benedict's Junior School, Ealing

The Bird

It's a high flyer in the air,
It's a diver in the air,
It's a swooping blur coming down,
It's plummeting down to Earth,
Hopping up from the cat,
Swooping down at the end of the day
To its bed on the hay.

Billy Oubridge (9)
St Benedict's Junior School, Ealing

Spring

Spring is coming,
The trees grow blossom,
Baby animals are born,
Daffodils grow,
Days get longer,
After Lent, it's Easter,
And lots of chocolate!

James Ball (7)
St Benedict's Junior School, Ealing

Families

Families all stay strong,
Families in which we belong.
Families undivided,
Those which are united.
My family is precious to me,
I wonder how yours might be?

Binath Philomin (8)
St Benedict's Junior School, Ealing

Koala

K ing of the outback
O bserving the scenery
A ll he can see
L ooking at me
A lone and dreamy.

Camena Foote (9)
St Benedict's Junior School, Ealing

Harry Potter

Harry Potter, Harry Potter,
Fighting Voldemort, the rotter,
Using magic wand and cloak
And spells to send him up in smoke.

Henry Weathersbee (8)
St Benedict's Junior School, Ealing

Valentine's Day

Today is St Valentine's Day
Love is in the air
All I want to say
Is I love you
In a very special way
I hope to be with you
Every second of the day
But will you come with me
Through a journey of love?
We will soar through the sky
We will never look behind
Except for the good times
And will you be mine
Happy Valentine's.

Krista Yaxley (9)
St John's CE Primary School, Penge

The Butterfly's Destiny

A butterfly flies through the baby-blue sky,
Light shining on its wing,
Making the most tiny reflection,
It's tired and goes to rest on a flower,
Drinking the pollen.
Breathing most quietly,
It gets up from its rest and continues its journey,
Fluttering from leaf to leaf,
Until it reaches its destiny.

India Barrett (7)
St John's CE Primary School, Penge

Poetry Explorers – South & West London

The New Pet

To Spikey,

It was that Sunday;
When I came home and there he lay,
Wagging his tail away and away.

He stretched his legs;
And opened his mouth like a peg,
Meanwhile he got up ready to play,
But instead he watched the TV all day.

Then it was dark;
And his eyes flickered like sparks,
'Time for bed!' we said,
And so he did!

Chloe Cornish (10)
St John's CE Primary School, Penge

Poems

Poems are funny.
Poems are sad.
Poems can be happy.
Poems can be long.
Poems can be short.
Some poems can rhyme.
The fun never ends when you are writing a poem.
Reading poems makes you improve your reading.
One thing is for sure, poems are fun to read.

Darius Xavier (7)
St John's CE Primary School, Penge

My Cat

With their grotty hairballs, cats can be a pest,
But my cat's sleek and ice-cool, much nicer than the rest,
My cat's not a tabby or a stupid tomcat,
Posh ones aren't too shabby but my cat's better than that!
My cat's black and beautiful, with small sparkling eyes,
Compared to yours he's wonderful, but, tough luck, he's mine!
My cat's practically perfect for going on holidays,
Your one's just not worth it, and he smells, by the way.
My cat never hunts for stupid rats or flies,
My cat's never won by chasing butterflies,
Erm, my cat isn't really like that, not lovely and black . . .
My cat's just a big-eyed, huggable tomcat!

Rachel Langford Honeysett (9)
St John's CE Primary School, Penge

The Rainbow Fairies

The rainbow fairies are never seen
Because they are protected by their king and queen,
They have celebrations
And pretty decorations,
They live in a palace with towers
And they each have secret powers,
Their enemy, Jack Frost, is nasty and cruel
But he thinks he can take over and rule,
The fairies fight with their magical glitter
And Jack Frost has gone all cold and bitter,
The fairies might come out at night
But be sure not to give them a fright!

Alana Hewitt (10)
St John's CE Primary School, Penge

Poetry Explorers – South & West London

Snow

S now normally happens once every two years,
N o school for the whole day,
O ver the country there is snow,
W hatever the time, town or weather, there may be a chance of
     Snow!
       Snow!
         Snow!
           Snow!
             Snow!
               Snow!
                 Snow!

Joseph Adusei
St John's CE Primary School, Penge

I Am The Owl

The moonlight shines on me as I fly,
Through the night, looking, watching, staring,
My eyes gleam as I look to the stars.

Snuffle, snuffle, I hear as a mouse runs by,
I grab it with my talons and take it to my babies.

You might think that owls are creepy creatures, killers,
But it's just our way of life, like yours to exterminate us, animals.
You are an evil, bigger threat to us than we are to you!

Clare Symons (11)
St John's CE Primary School, Penge

Things I Like

I love to learn and make things
and do everything at school.
I love playing with my friends
and maths, best of all.
The best of all is everybody at St John's.
St John's school is a family.

Ella Robertson
St John's CE Primary School, Penge

My Kitten

Talullah is small but very cute,
I love her so much, now that's the truth,
Guess what?
She is my kitten.

Olivia Tizie (9)
St John's CE Primary School, Penge

Smile

S unny days
M ountains of smiles
I ncredible looks that make me smile
L aughter of joy
E cstatic moments that make me go wild!

Alicia Treleven (11)
St John's CE Primary School, Walworth

Phantom Manor

(Inspired by the ride 'Phantom Manor')

Over a rotten hill
Past the old mill
There was the Manor
Phantom Manor . . .

Spooks and ghouls come to life
And avenge the beautiful, dead wife
Heaven and Hell come together
Create destruction altogether.

The graveyard gates open
Out comes the groom
He walked into the dark room
Cobwebs and dim lights
It was almost twilight.

Ghost and ghouls come to life
And avenge the beautiful, dead wife
Heaven and Hell come together
Create destruction altogether.

Enter the prison
And be sentenced to crucifixion
Life becomes death
And death becomes life.

Ghost and ghouls come to life
And avenge the beautiful, dead wife
Heaven and Hell come together
Create destruction altogether.

Ghost and ghouls come to life
And avenge the beautiful, dead wife
Heaven and Hell come together
And create destruction altogether.

Ben Fox (11)
St John's CE Primary School, Walworth

Anger Makes Me Feel . . .

Anger is a furious feeling,
It is like a hot volcano,
That is about to erupt.
When you are angry,
The blood inside of you,
Rushes to your head dangerously
And then you suddenly explode.

Anger makes you violent,
Like a lion fighting a wild bear,
You start to grow claws and sharp teeth
And then you become a giant . . .
Monster!
Your heart beats vigorously
And then you become a giant beast.

Anger makes you roar and growl,
It is a pouncing leopard,
That eventually found its predator
And then when the anger grabs hold of you,
It's anger that you can't control.
You start screaming mentally,
Then your neighbour asks, 'What's happening?'

Anger is taking illegal drugs,
That gets you into prison or jail,
The rage in you,
Breaks all your bones
And then you feel like fire.
You start to boil like a hot kettle
And you do all these things, just because you're . . .
Angry!

Gift Okonkwo (11)
St John's CE Primary School, Walworth

Poetry Explorers — South & West London

Love

Love is a sacred flame
That burns eternally.
No one can dim the special glow,
Or change my love for you.

When I'm at my weakest point,
You tell me to continue the race.
You are my sun, moon and stars,
Without you, my world is full of darkness.

You are an important piece
Of the circuit in my life,
Without you, my heart won't beat,
Just like a bulb won't light.
You're on my mind,
Day and night,
Your gentle hug and gracious smile,
I thank God for sending a loving person like you.

I can truly say, *you* are the angel in my life, *mum!*

Tamara Ajudua (11)
St John's CE Primary School, Walworth

Love

If I could have just one wish,
I would wish to wake up to,
The birds singing,
Listening to their sweet, sweet, voice,
It just lightens my day.

You know why,
Because whenever I look at the birds,
I am lost in their magic,
They light up my life,
As my heart beats crazily in my chest!

I love them with all my
Heart, body, soul and mind,
I love the way they sing,
They are like my family,
Or my favourite song or film!

Tyanna McLean (11)
St John's CE Primary School, Walworth

Wonderland

White clouds, fluffy and sweet,
God's creatures, big and so petite,
Birds in deep blue sky, going tweet, tweet,
Sun shining down, feels like I can touch the sky,
Waterfalls, sunsets and rainbows,
Blue, calming, relaxing waves,
Sand like golden salt,
It looks like glitter was sprinkled on the seashores,
Exotic sunshine from skies above,
Natural enclosure so tender and sweet,
Romantic and beautiful night falls,
The sun goes down, the stars come out,
So pretty and proud.

Tosin Sokoya (10)
St John's CE Primary School, Walworth

Dance

Booty shaking
Head nodding
Popping, locking
Flicking, ticking
Face expressions
Funky costumes
Highly confident
Maximum attitude
Complicated routines
Different styles.

Paris McLean (10)
St John's CE Primary School, Walworth

The Sea

The sea is like the sky,
It covers the world,
The fish in the sea are like the clouds
In the sky.

The fish roam through the sea,
They swim through its currents,
With their tiny fins,
Swimming forever.

The sea makes a sound like a curtain swishing,
The waves rise up,
The waves crash back down,
And they hit the sand.

Brian Asiedu-Obiri (11)
St John's CE Primary School, Walworth

My Sister

Eliza, always happy as the sun appearing
From behind a cloud
TV is like the cinema for her
Going out and about is like a trip around the world
Eyes as blue as the sea
Hair as yellow as buttercups
Skin as pink as roses
Known her forever
She is my sister.

Millie Price (8)
Sheen Mount School, Sheen

I Wish...

I wish I could see deep into someone's anger
To find out how to fix it
I wish I could travel to the future to see if we will survive
Or if not, to be on our guard
I wish I could phone someone
Then travel through the telephone wire to see them
I wish I could have magic powers
I wish I could make people happy always
I wish I could sit on a cloud to see if I would fall
I wish I could taste a moonbeam to find out what it tastes like
I wish I could find all the missing people
And put the kidnappers in jail
I wish I could control the weather.

Georgina Russell (8)
Sheen Mount School, Sheen

The Sun

The sun is hot,
It's like it lives in a sizzling pot,
Nearer and nearer it comes every day,
Sometimes you want it to go away!
Boiling, sizzling, very shiny,
But from below, it looks very tiny,
Soon, soon, it comes, you see,
Sometimes, it will talk to me!

Harriet Groves (8)
Sheen Mount School, Sheen

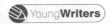

Untitled

Pandas are cute
Pandas are cool
Pandas are funny
Pandas are the best
Pandas are fat
Pandas are black and white
Pandas are strong
Pandas are chubby
Pandas are big
Pandas are short
Pandas are tricky
Pandas are adorable
Pandas are quiet.

Vincent Wong
Stockwell Primary School, Lambeth

I Have...

I have a sister
I have a mum
I have a house
I have a garden
I have a school
I have love
I have a teacher
I have a policeman
I have a brother
I have a carpet.

Osman Sihaam
Stockwell Primary School, Lambeth

I Went To School

I woke up
I had a bath
I wore my clothes
I ate my food
I went to school
I did my work
I went to lunch
I played outside
I did my work
I went home
I had my tea
I went to bed.

Rasidatu Bisuga (6)
Stockwell Primary School, Lambeth

Happiness

H appy
A nything to do
P eaceful
P laying
I n love
N ice and comfortable
E nchanting
S o, so happy
S uch a joy
   This is happiness!

Aaron Ormsby
Stockwell Primary School, Lambeth

Happy Life – Haikus

Today is happy
I am getting a hamster
I will play all day

Legoland is fun
Legoland's cool and fun
Happy, happy fun

Beach is very hot
Hot and fun and hot and fun
Very hot, hot, hot!

Mateusz Matczak (9)
Stockwell Primary School, Lambeth

Life

Life is peaceful
Life is nice
People have a great time
Life is great
Life is fantastic
Children having fun
Life is beautiful
Life is high spirits
And that's why I love life.

Fahima Khatun
Stockwell Primary School, Lambeth

I Am School

I am sad
I am happy
I am mad
I am tired
I am hungry
I am angry
I am thin
I am serious.

Jamith Horna
Stockwell Primary School, Lambeth

Unicorn

Unicorn
Fantasy animal
White, silky, special
Long white horn, magical
Shiny as a star
Nice, wonderful
Mysterious.

Rachel Wong (9)
Stockwell Primary School, Lambeth

World

The world is great
The world is peaceful
There is love in the world
People love the world
The world is a beauty
Shout out to the world
It's a great place to be!

Aaliya Mohamed
Stockwell Primary School, Lambeth

Life

Life is your spirit of love
Life makes your soul free
Life has incredible miracles
Life is loving each other
Life makes you have nature
Life has love of our creator, Jesus.

Diogo
Stockwell Primary School, Lambeth

Poetry Explorers – South & West London

Rain

R unning along the stream
A ll of a sudden, splishing and splashing
I mportant rain is useful
N ever get dirty rain on yourself.

Nadiyah Hazari
Stockwell Primary School, Lambeth

Whatever The Weather

Whatever the weather
Rain or sun, Heather
Just hated the weather,

Whatever the weather
Snow or cold, Heather
Hated saying the word weather,

Whatever the weather
Wind or fog, Heather
Did not think about the weather,

Whatever the weather
Thunder or storm, Heather
Thought that the weather
Was boring,

Whatever the weather
Chilly or burning, Heather
Was not so more interested in the weather,
Years passed, Heather did like the weather,
But not so much!

Ahlam Nur (9)
Sulivan Primary School, Fulham

Snow

Snow falls around us,
Snow is on the bus,
Snow falls on the ground,
You could never find a pound.

Snow falls from the sky,
Birds fly way up high,
Snow surrounds my feet,
People crunching through the street.

Snowflakes fall from the air,
Snowflakes sit on your chair,
Snow finds its place on your coat,
Finds its place on a boat.

If you say ice,
They will say no,
If you get blown away,
Don't blame me for your day!

Hoda Tarmach (8)
Sulivan Primary School, Fulham

Poor Little Boy

There is a little boy, a poor little orphan,
He has no mum or no one to talk to,
He is very lonely and he has no life,
Now he just wants to end his dull, ugly life.

He touches the unhygienic pavement,
The poor, miserable boy hears the things he shouldn't hear,
His nose smells chemicals flying out of cigarettes,
While he thinks about the things that he regrets.

His life is as bad as the ghosts that he believes in,
His education is so useless, you might as well throw it in the bin,
His bravery has been worn out since five years ago in September.

Then, one day, someone came along and asked
If he wanted to run along,
He said no, but she dragged him along,
Then he lived a happy life
And his future was a very happy sight.

Samuel James Constanti (9)
Sulivan Primary School, Fulham

Little Santa

Little Santa walking down the street,
Snow crunching when he stamps his feet,
He tripped on a lady and fell into some thorns,
The lady dropped her prawns.

Little Santa shouted, 'Ow!'
He went to the doctor, right now,
The doctor started pulling thorns out,
Little Santa had to shout!

He finished at last and he ran home fast,
He saw dancing bananas in pyjamas,
He fainted in shock,
'What a day it's been!' he said.

Amal Jama (8)
Sulivan Primary School, Fulham

Water Dragon

A fire dragon is a light,
He doesn't even go to sleep at night.
A dragon's flame is stronger than a clown,
He never has a big frown.

A dragon's sense is very good,
He can smell a person's foot.
A water dragon has filthy feet,
He doesn't even have to fold his clothes neat.

The water dragon, so stuck up,
The fire dragon wants to eat him up!

Jonathan Kyle (7)
Sulivan Primary School, Fulham

# Poetry Explorers – South & West London

Roses

The rose is crystal clean, as a new shoe
When the wind blows, it sways
The rose is as white as snow
What a sight in white
What a sight in green grass and roses.

She is as much fun as a dog
She is like a ballerina
She loves the fresh air.

Oh! I am weak
Oh no! You are dying
I went to get water
Next, *snap!* She had died.

Angel Lawal (7)
Sulivan Primary School, Fulham

Bugs

Scorpions have a sting in their tails
Female black widows eat all the males
A caterpillar turns into a butterfly
A praying mantis is an insect Samurai
Ladybirds are red with black spots
Try to count a millipede's legs, they have lots
A cockroach can live for two weeks without its head
Ten giant leeches sucking your blood, can make you dead
Bugs are amazing and interesting creatures
And there are a lot of things they could teach us!

James Gent (10)
Sulivan Primary School, Fulham

Bonfire Fire

Bright yellow, red, orange fire
Burns like your dinner in the oven.

The colour of the fireworks
Are better than the colours of the rainbow.

I love the fireworks!

So why don't you come on down and have a laugh
But first, you have to have a bath.

The fireworks go *bang! Crash!*
But Mummy, I need some cash
Before I go, *smash! Smash! Smash!*

Brooke Blagrove (9)
Sulivan Primary School, Fulham

Los Angeles

L A
O h, how I love LA
S uperstars out there

A merican Idol
N ow everybody listen up, we're coming your way
G reat restaurants in each area
E verybody welcome
L ive music every night
E vening dinner waiting for you
S leep tight and goodnight!

Indiana Fofie-Collins (8)
The Priory CE Primary School, Wimbledon

Do Not Fear Me

I'm in a new world
With nothing the same.
Everyone hits me
And makes fun of my name.
Maybe they fear me
More than I fear them.
Please do not fear me
And you'll be my friend.
Now I am friends
And can talk about home
And the reason I'm here
And was all on my own.
My friend understands
And was once just like me.
So if you could
Leave and let us be.
We talk about secrets
And all that we miss.
We both miss the sun
And the blazing hot sand.
We both miss our houses
And gardens, of course.
But we're the same as you
So do not fear us.

Joe Sansom (9)
The Priory CE Primary School, Wimbledon

Chinese Whispers

C hildren play all over the world
H appiness is the game
I ntelligence is all you need
N o words said out loud till the end
E verybody joins in
S ome funny things are said
E ither way, no one wins

W ith more people in the circle it grows
H ow many different words can be changed
I nspire yourself with magical words
S oftly say the words
P eople wait until their turn
E xcitement as it comes
R ound and round the words flow
S ecrets crawl through your ear.

Devendra Bathia (9)
The Priory CE Primary School, Wimbledon

Winter

Face slapper
Finger pincher
Frost painter
Snow bringer
Water freezer
Guess what season it is?

Kyle Sterling (8)
The Priory CE Primary School, Wimbledon

Beach

Beach crowding
Sun blistering
Sand crumbling
Wave curling
Surfers dodging
Deckchair collapsing
Ice cream dripping
Children digging
Mums chatting
Rain showering
People fleeing
Beach deserting
Back to school.

Gabriel Tweedale (9)
The Priory CE Primary School, Wimbledon

I Walked Home From School One Day

I walked home from school one day
And got caught in a big delay
For people had chosen
To watch Michael Rosen
And hear what he had to say.

Joseph Digger (8)
The Priory CE Primary School, Wimbledon

Seashore — Haiku

Whooshing, crashing waves
Foamy sand against the shore
That is a seashore.

Kayleigh Spencer Smyth (8)
The Priory CE Primary School, Wimbledon

Young Writers Information

We hope you have enjoyed reading this book - and that you will continue to enjoy it in the coming years.

If you like reading and writing poetry drop us a line, or give us a call, and we'll send you a free information pack.

Alternatively if you would like to order further copies of this book or any of our other titles, then please give us a call or log onto our website at www.youngwriters.co.uk

Young Writers Information
Remus House
Coltsfoot Drive
Peterborough
PE2 9JX
(01733) 890066